Julie Brook

CW01501656

PUBLISHED BY: Jul
Copyright © 2016 All rig

Contents

Free Gift

If you would like to receive a free gift – my Top 100 Cupcake Recipes – then please just enter your email address here:

http://eepurl.com/bWd-XL

and I will send it off to you right now.

I would love to be able to send you news about my latest books and delicious recipes for you to enjoy.

Introduction

Welcome to the Top 50 Sheet cake, bar and squares cookbook! This cookbook contains the best 50 recipes for baking a cake in a sheet pan or jelly roll pan.

A sheet cake, also known as a tray bake, might just about be the best dessert you can make for friends or family. It is extremely easy to create, takes very little time and is enjoyed by all. It is ideal for parties, it can be cut up into whatever size slices feels right and can be carried around outside or from one room to the next without fear of depositing it on the floor in a sorry mess. A sheet cake is truly the easiest and most efficient way to get everyone in the room eating your cake!

They are also easy to decorate and look stunning. You can have a huge variety of icings and toppings on your sheet cake and it's adored by children and adults alike. This book covers whole sheet cakes and bars and squares as well, so you will find something here for everyone.

This book is the ultimate resource for sheet cakes, bars and squares. With 50 of the best recipes in one location, this book will provide you will all the recipes you need to keep your family and friends happy for any occasion.

Read on now for the recipes and happy baking!

Julie

Almond Squares

Ingredients

1 cup butter

½ cup sugar

2 eggs

½ cup almond paste

1 teaspoon almond extract

1 teaspoon vanilla

2 cups all-purpose flour

2 ½ ounces almonds

Directions

Prepare a 13x9 pan by greasing the inside and adding parchment paper. Add the butter into a bowl and cream. Add the sugar slowly and beat until fluffy. Separate the egg yolks from the whites and add the yolk, almond paste, almond extract and vanilla extract and beat everything together. Add in flour and stir in.

Add the mixture to the prepared pan. Beat the remaining egg white and then spread it over the top of pan. Add the sliced almonds on top. Bake for 30 minutes or until golden brown. Remove, allow to cool and cut into squares to serve.

Apple Pie Bars

These look and taste great and are perfect for any slightly old apples you may have around. Use them up with this apple recipe.

Ingredients

1 cup butter

3 large apples

½ cup butter

1 teaspoon apple pie sauce

1 ½ cups sugar

4 eggs

3 teaspoons vanilla

2 cups all-purpose flour

½ teaspoon salt

Directions

Preheat the oven to 350F and prepare a 13x9 inch pan by greasing or with cooking spray. Peel and dice the applies and add ½ cup butter, the tablespoons of sugar and apple pie sauce to a pan. Sauté the apples until they're very soft and set aside.

Melt the butter over a low heat and set aside to cool. Add the sugar, eggs and vanilla to a bowl and whisk together. Slowly stir in the flour and salt. Now add the apple mix. Add the batter to the pan with some sugar on top for a glaze and cook for about 25 minutes. Remove and allow to cool in the pan. Slice and serve.

Banana Sheet Cake

A delicious cake that is perfect for banana lovers – these won't be around for long.

Ingredients

2 cups all-purpose flour

½ teaspoon salt

2 teaspoons cinnamon

1 teaspoon baking soda

½ cup unsalted butter

3 eggs

1 cup sugar

1 ½ teaspoon vanilla extract

1 ½ cup of ripe bananas

½ cup sour cream

Frosting

1 (8oz) cream cheese

¼ cup of butter

3 cups powdered sugar

2 teaspoon vanilla

Directions

Preheat the oven to 350F and grease your 13x9 tin. Add the flour, baking soda, cinnamon and salt into a bowl, mix together and set aside. In a different bowl mix the sugar and butter together. Add in the eggs, one at a time, beating each one in and then add the vanilla and mashed up bananas.

Add in the flour mixture from the other bowl and then the sour cream and mix together. Pour into your pan and cook for a little over 20 minutes. You are looking to get a lovely brown color on top. Remove and allow to cool for an hour or so.

For the frosting, add the butter to the cream cheese and beat. Add the powdered sugar and vanilla, mix in and then frost the cake to serve.

Brownie Bars

Ingredients

1 cup butter

4 ounces semi-sweet chocolate

1 ½ cups sugar

4 eggs

1 ½ cups all-purpose flour

1/3 cup unsweetened cocoa powder

½ teaspoon salt

Directions

Preheat the oven to 350F and prepare a 13x9 inch pan by greasing or with cooking spray. Melt the butter and chocolate together either in the microwave or in a glass bowl over a saucepan of boiling water. Once it has cooled a little stir in the sugar and eggs. Add the flour, cocoa powder and salt and whisk together. Pour the batter into your pan and bake for about 30 minutes. Remove from oven and allow to cool before slicing and serving.

Butterscotch Bars

Ingredients

½ cup butter

1 ½ cups brown sugar

1 ½ cups all-purpose flour

2 teaspoons baking powder

½ teaspoon salt

2 eggs

1 teaspoon vanilla extract

1 cup

1 cup chopped nuts (optional)

Directions

Preheat the oven to 350F and prepare a 13x9 inch pan by greasing or with cooking spray. Add the flour, baking powder and salt into a bowl and mix together. Add the butter and sugar to a saucepan and melt together over a low heat. Add in flour mixture, followed by the eggs and vanilla. At this point, you can also add in the chopped nuts.

Bake for about 20 minutes and remove to cut and serve.

Caramel Bars

Ingredients

50 caramels

6 tablespoons heavy cream

1 cup all-purpose flour

2 cups rolled oats

1 cup brown sugar

½ teaspoon baking soda

1 ½ cup butter

½ cup semisweet chocolate chips

Directions

Preheat the oven to 350F and prepare a 13x9 inch pan by greasing or with cooking spray. Melt the butter in a microwave. Add the unwrapped caramels into a saucepan and heat with heavy cream. In a separate bowl add the flour, oats, sugar and baking soda. Add in the butter and stir together. Place half of this mixture into your pan and bake for about 10 minutes first.

Now add the chocolate chips in (you can omit this if you don't want it quite so sweet) and then pour the caramel mixture over the top. Finally, add the remaining flour mixture over the top. It should just sink into the mixture, but you can press down lightly with a spatula if it doesn't quite embed into the caramel.

Place the pan back into the oven and cook for another 15 minutes or until it is golden. Remove from heat and allow to cool a little before cutting into squares to serve.

Carrot Cake Bars

Ingredients

1 ½ cups sugar

1 ½ cups vegetable oil

2 cups all-purpose flour

4 eggs

2 teaspoons baking soda

4 teaspoons cinnamon

1 teaspoon salt

2 cups baby carrots

½ cup raisins

Directions

Preheat the oven to 350F and prepare a 15x10 inch pan by greasing or with cooking spray. Steam the carrots and then add to a blender. Puree until smooth and put to one side. Add the flour, baking soda, cinnamon and salt to a bowl and mix together. In a separate bowl, beat together the sugar, eggs and oil. Add in the flour mix, followed by the carrots and then the raisins, stirring after each addition.

Pour the batter into the pan and bake for about 20 minutes or until a toothpick comes out clean. Remove and cool before cutting into squares to serve.

Cherry Squares

These are great in little squares, but very more-ish. Give them a go today and see for yourself.

Ingredients

2 ½ cups all-purpose flour

2/3 cup brown sugar

1 cup butter

4 eggs

2 ½ cups brown sugar

1 teaspoon baking powder

¼ teaspoon salt

2 cups flaked coconut

1 cup maraschino cherries

1 cup powdered sugar

2 tablespoons butter

1 teaspoon vanilla

1 tablespoon cherry juice

Directions

Preheat the oven to 350F and prepare a 13x9 inch pan by greasing or with cooking spray. Add 2 ½ cups of flour and 2/3 cup brown sugar into a bowl and then add the cup of butter. Mix together and then spread the mixture into the pan. Bake for 15 minutes and then remove to cool.

In a separate bowl add the eggs and beat. Add in the brown sugar, flour, baking powder and salt and stir. Add in the coconut and cherries and spread over the pan. Place in the oven and bake for 30 minutes or until golden brown. Remove and allow to cool.

For the topping, add the powdered sugar, butter, vanilla and the cherry juice into a bowl and mix until the consistency is perfect. Spread over the baked bars and then cut into small pieces to serve.

Cherry-Choc Bars

Ingredients

1 cup butter

¾ cup granulated sugar

3 eggs

2 ½ cups all-purpose flour

1 teaspoon baking soda

½ teaspoon salt

1 teaspoon vanilla

½ teaspoon almond extract

1 cup semi-sweet chocolate chips

1 cup dried cherries

Directions

Preheat the oven to 350F and prepare a 13x9 inch pan by greasing or with cooking spray.

Add the flour, baking soda and salt into a bowl and set aside. Beat the butter, sugars, vanilla and almond extracts in another bowl until fluffy. Add the eggs separately, beating after each addition. Beat in the flour mixture and then add chocolate chips and the chopped dried cherries. Stir and then add the batter to the pan.

Bake for about 25 minutes and then remove to cool. Cut into squares and serve.

Choc Chip Cookie Bars

Ingredients

3 cups all-purpose flour

1 teaspoon baking soda

1 teaspoon salt

1 cup butter

¾ cup sugar, granulated

¾ cup brown sugar

2 teaspoons vanilla

3 eggs

1 ½ cups semi-sweet choc chips

Directions

Preheat the oven to 350F and prepare a 13x9 inch pan by greasing or with cooking spray. Add the flour, baking soda and salt into a bowl and set aside. Beat the butter, sugars and vanilla in another bowl until fluffy. Add the eggs separately, beating after each addition. Beat in the flour mixture and then add chocolate chips. Stir and then add the batter to the pan.

Bake for about 20 minutes and then remove to cool. Cut into squares to suit and serve!

Choc Oat No Bake Bars

Ingredients

1 ½ cups butter

1 cup brown sugar

2 teaspoons vanilla

5 cups quick oats

1 ½ cups semisweet chocolate chips

¾ cup peanut butter

Directions

Prepare a 13x9 pan by greasing the inside. Add the butter to a saucepan and melt over a low heat. Add brown sugar and vanilla and stir. Mix in oats and cook until everything is blended together. Add half of the mixture into the pan and press down firmly to compact.

In another pan, add the chocolate chips and peanut butter and heat until a smooth texture is reached. Add this to the pan over the top of the crust and spread with a spatula.

Add the remaining oaty mix over the top and press down. Add to the fridge for a few hours and remove to cut into squares and serve.

Chocolate Banana Bars

Ingredients

3 cups all-purpose flour

1 teaspoon salt

1 cup butter

¾ cup sugar, granulated

¾ cup brown sugar

2 teaspoons vanilla

1 large mashed banana

3 eggs

½ cup chocolate hazelnut spread

Directions

Preheat the oven to 350F and prepare a 13x9 inch pan by greasing or with cooking spray. Add the flour and salt into a bowl and set aside. Beat the butter, sugars, mashed banana and vanilla in another bowl until fluffy. Add the eggs separately, beating after each addition. Beat in the flour mixture and then add chocolate chips. Stir and then add the batter to the pan. Finally, add the chocolate hazelnut spread into the batter in the pan and mix around.

Bake for about 30 minutes and then remove to cool. Cut into squares and serve!

Chocolate Brownie Bars

Ingredients

1 ½ cups sugar

5 eggs

½ cup vegetable oil

2 teaspoons vanilla

2 cups all-purpose flour

½ cup cocoa powder

1 teaspoon salt

1 ½ cups semisweet chocolate chips

Directions

Preheat oven to 350F. Prepare a 13x9 pan by greasing the inside. Add the sugar, eggs, oil and vanilla into a bowl and mix together. In a separate bowl add the flour, cocoa and salt and mix together. Add the flour mixture to the egg mixture gradually. Add the chocolate chips to the mixture and stir. Pour the batter into the pan and bake for 35 minutes.

Remove and allow to cool before cutting into squares to serve.

Chocolate Mint Bars

Ingredients

½ cup butter

1 cup sugar

1 can chocolate syrup (16 ounce)

4 eggs

1 teaspoon vanilla

½ teaspoon salt

1 cup powdered sugar

½ cup butter

1 ½ teaspoon mint extract

1 cup semisweet chocolate chips

5 tablespoons butter

Directions

Preheat oven to 350F. Prepare a 13x9 pan by greasing the inside. Add the sugar and butter into a bowl and mix together. Add the eggs separately and beat after each addition. In a different bowl add the flour and salt and mix together. Combine this with the egg mix and pour into the pan. Bake for 20-25 minutes, remove from the oven and allow to cool.

In a new bowl, add the second ½ cup of butter and powdered sugar and beat together. Add the mint extract and spread over the pan. Remove and let it cool.

Finally, melt the chocolate chips and butter together either over a low heat or in the microwave. Spread over the brownies and let it cool again. Once cooled, cut into small squares to serve.

Cinnamon Maple Bars

Ingredients

1 cup butter

¾ cup granulated sugar

½ cup maple syrup

3 eggs

2 ½ cups all-purpose flour

1 teaspoon baking soda

½ teaspoon salt

1 teaspoon vanilla

½ teaspoon maple extract

1 cup cinnamon baking chips

Directions

Preheat the oven to 350F and prepare a 13x9 inch pan by greasing or with cooking spray.

Add the flour, baking soda and salt into a bowl and set aside. Beat the butter, sugars, maple syrup, vanilla and maple extract in another bowl until fluffy. Add the eggs separately, beating after each addition. Beat in the flour mixture and then add cinnamon baking chips. Stir and then add the batter to the pan.

Bake for about 20 minutes and then remove to cool. Cut into whatever size squares takes your fancy and enjoy

Classic Blondies Bars

Ingredients

1 cup butter

2 cups light brown sugar

2 eggs

2 tablespoons vanilla

2 ½ cups all-purpose flour

¼ teaspoon salt

½ teaspoon baking soda

1 cup butterscotch chips

Directions

Preheat the oven to 350F and prepare a 13x9 inch pan by greasing or with cooking spray. Melt the butter and allow to cool a little. Add the sugar, eggs and vanilla together and whisk. Add in the flour, baking soda and salt and stir. Add in the butterscotch chips and stir.

Pour the batter into the pan and bake for 40 minutes or until a toothpick comes out clean. Remove, allow to cool and cut to serve.

Coconut and Chocolate Chip Bars

Ingredients

½ cup butter

2 cups light brown sugar

2 eggs

2 teaspoons vanilla

½ teaspoon salt

1 teaspoon baking powder

1 cup all-purpose flour

2 cups flaked coconut

1 cup semisweet chocolate chips

Directions

Preheat the oven to 350F and prepare a 13x9 inch pan by greasing or with cooking spray. Melt the butter and add in the brown sugar over a gentle heat. Continue to stir until it has all combined. Remove from the heat. Stir in the vanilla, eggs, salt and baking powder. Add the mixture to a bowl.

Gradually spoon in the flour, followed by the coconut and lastly the chocolate chips stirring throughout. Pour the batter into the pan and bake for about 20 minutes or until you get a golden brown on top. Remove from the heat, cool and cut into squares to serve.

Cola Sheet Cake

Ingredients

2 cups all-purpose flour

1 cup sugar

1/3 cup cocoa powder

1 teaspoon baking soda

½ teaspoon salt

½ cup vegetable oil

1 cup cola

1/3 cup buttermilk

1 teaspoon vanilla

Icing

½ cup unsalted butter

¼ cup unsweetened cocoa powder

1/3 cup cola

Pinch of salt

2 cups powdered sugar

Chopped nuts (optional)

Directions

Preheat the oven to 350F and prepare a 10x15 inch pan by greasing or with cooking spray. Add the flour, sugar, cocoa, baking soda and salt in a bowl and stir together. Set the bowl to one side. In a separate bowl, whisk the oil, buttermilk and vanilla together. Add the wet ingredients to the dry and stir.

Pour the batter into the pan and bake for about 20 minutes or until the toothpick comes out clean. Remove and allow to cool.

For the icing, add the butter, cocoa and cola into a saucepan until boiling point is reached. Take off the heat and add the vanilla, salt and sugar. Spread over the cake and add some type of decorative garnish such as chopped nuts if you wish to serve.

Cranberry Squares

Ingredients

½ cup sugar

2 cups all-purpose flour

2 teaspoons baking powder

¼ teaspoon salt

1 egg

¾ cup butter

2 cups cranberry sauce

Directions

Preheat the oven to 350F and prepare a 13x9 inch pan by greasing or with cooking spray. Add the sugar, flour, salt and baking powder into a bowl and mix together. Add in the butter that is cut into small pieces and then stir in the egg.

Set half the mixture to one side and then add the other half into the pan. Press down on the mixture with your hands so it is tight in the pan. Add the cranberry sauce on top and then add the other half of the mixture on top. Press down lightly with your hands.

Place the pan back into the oven and cook for another 35 minutes or until it is golden. Remove from heat and allow to cool before cutting into squares to serve.

Cream Cheese Sheet Cake

Ingredients

1 cup butter

2 packets (3 ounces) cream cheese

2 cups sugar

6 eggs

1 teaspoon vanilla extract

2 cups all-purpose flour

Icing

1 cup sugar

1/3 cup evaporated milk

½ cup butter

½ cup chocolate chips

Directions

Preheat the oven to 350F and prepare a 15x10 inch pan by greasing. Add the butter, cream cheese and sugar into a large bowl and beat together. Add eggs separately and beat with each one. Add in the vanilla, followed by the flour and combine. Pour the batter into your pan and cook for 30 minutes or until the toothpick comes out clean. Remove and allow to cool.

To make the icing, add the sugar and milk into a saucepan and bring to the boil. Let it cook there for three minutes and then add in the butter and choc chips. Once everything has melted, remove, let it cool and spread over the top of the cake.

Date Bars

Ingredients

1 ½ cups rolled oats

1 cup all-purpose flour

1 teaspoon baking soda

½ cup butter

½ pound pitted dates

½ cup brown sugar

1 cup water

1 teaspoon lemon juice

Directions

Preheat the oven to 350F and prepare a 9x9 inch pan by greasing or with cooking spray. Add the oats, flour, brown sugar and baking soda into a bowl and mix together. Place half the mixture into the bottom of the pan. Bake the bottom half for about 10 minutes and then remove from the oven.

While baking, chop the dates up into small pieces. Add the dates with the water and lemon juice into a pan and bring to the boil. Remove from the heat and pour over the 9x9 pan. Now add the second half of the mix over the dates.

Place the pan back into the oven and cook for another 15 minutes or until it is golden. Remove from heat and allow to cool before cutting into squares to serve.

Funfetti Bars

Ingredients

1 box vanilla cake mix

¼ cup vegetable oil

1 egg

½ cup milk

½ cup sprinkles

1 cup white chocolate chips

Directions

Preheat the oven to 350F and prepare a 9x9 inch pan by greasing or with cooking spray. Add the cake mix, egg, oil and milk into a bowl and mix together. Pour the batter into the pan and then add the sprinkles and chocolate chips and stir them in.

Bake for about 30 minutes or until you get a golden brown on top. Remove from the heat, cool and cut into squares to serve.

Ginger Cake

Ingredients

1 ½ cups brown sugar

1 cup butter

¼ cup molasses

3 teaspoons ginger

2 eggs

2 teaspoons vanilla

½ teaspoon clove

2 cups all-purpose flour

1 teaspoon baking powder

¼ teaspoon baking soda

½ teaspoon salt

Directions

Preheat oven to 350F. Prepare a 13x9 pan by greasing the inside. Add the sugar, butter and molasses into a bowl and combine. Add in the ginger, clove, eggs and vanilla. In another bowl, add the flour, baking soda, baking soda and salt. Add the flour mix gradually into the butter mix. Add the batter into the pan.

Bake for 35 minutes or until the toothpick comes out clean. Remove and let it cool before cutting into squares to serve.

Lemony Lemon Sheet Cake

There are a number of ways of making this sheet cake and I've tried most of them, but if you want to keep it simple and quick, it's hard to beat this one. I love lemon and the clean citrus taste it brings after a meal rounds everything off beautifully. Make a couple of these – they will go fast.

Ingredients

1 (18.25 oz) lemon cake mix

3 eggs

1 (15.75 oz) lemon pie filling

Frosting

1 (8oz) cream cheese

¼ cup of butter

3 cups powdered sugar

2 teaspoon vanilla

Directions

Once you've preheated the oven, then add the cake mix together with the eggs and mix. Prepare a 15x10x1 inch pan by greasing it and optionally adding aluminium foil as well. Now fold in your pie filling and pour into the egg mix. Add the lot to the pan and cook for about 20 minutes.

While that's cooling for an hour or so, you can make the frosting. Just add the cream cheese and butter together and beat. Add the powdered sugar now with the vanilla and if you're sure the cake has cooled, go ahead and frost it. A perfect summery, light treat!

Marble Sheet Cake

Ingredients

3 cups all-purpose flour

1 tablespoon baking powder

½ teaspoon salt

1 ½ cups sugar

1 cup butter

4 eggs

2 teaspoons vanilla

1 cup milk

¼ cup unsweetened cocoa

3 tablespoons water

Icing

½ cup butter

3 cups powdered sugar

2/3 cup unsweetened cocoa

3 tablespoons milk

1 teaspoon vanilla

Directions

Preheat the oven to 350F and prepare a 15x10 inch pan by greasing or with cooking spray. Add the flour, baking powder and salt to a bowl and put to one side. Add the sugar and butter into a separate bowl and beat. Add the eggs one at a time, beating again each time.

Add the vanilla, followed by half the flour, half the milk, the remaining flour and lastly the remaining milk. Beat the mixture each time you add.

Remove 2 cups of batter into another bowl into which you should add ¼ cup sugar, ¼ cup of cocoa and the water. Stir it all together.

To get the marble effect, add ¾ of the normal batter into the pan. Then add the chocolate batter on top followed by the remaining normal batter. Bake for about 25 minutes or until a toothpick comes out clean. Remove and allow to cool.

For the icing, place the butter in a bowl and beat until fluffy. Slowly beat in the sugar, cocoa, milk and vanilla. Spread over the cooled cake and serve.

Moist Carrot Sheet Cake and Frosting

The secret of any successful carrot cake is to ensure it remains moist. A dry carrot cake, even if smothered in frosting, will not prove popular. This recipe doesn't have any raisins in it as I'm not a great fan of them in carrot cake myself, but do add them of course if you prefer them. Here are the details

Ingredients

9 ounces all-purpose flour

2 teaspoons cinnamon

2 teaspoons baking powder

4 eggs

1 teaspoon salt

1 teaspoon baking soda

1 ½ teaspoon vanilla

½ cup vegetable oil

1 cup granulated sugar

2 pounds grated carrot

Smooth Chocolate Sheet Cake

Peanut Sheet Cake

Pumpkin Sheet Cake

Frosting

1 (8oz) cream cheese

¼ cup of butter

3 cups powdered sugar

2 teaspoon vanilla

Directions

This recipe calls for the 13x9 dish. Grease the pan or cover in aluminium foil if you prefer. Preheat the oven to 350 F. Beat together the oil and sugar and then add the flour and eggs. Beat again until everything is just about mixed. Gradually fold in all of the grated carrot until everything is fully mixed.

Add the mixture into a baking dish and bake for about 45 minutes. Remove and let it cool for around an hour. For the frosting, add the butter to the cream cheese and beat. The butter is optional if you'd prefer just to go with the cream cheese. Add the powdered sugar and vanilla, mix in and then frost the cake to serve.

Molasses with Ginger Bars

These are a lovely flavour which are popular all year, but very much so during the winter months when they come into their own. You can add chocolate chips to these as well if you like for another variety.

Ingredients

1 cup butter

½ cups sugar

½ cup light brown sugar

½ cup molasses

4 eggs

3 teaspoons vanilla

2 cups all-purpose flour

1 teaspoon ground ginger

1 teaspoon cinnamon

1 teaspoon ground nutmeg

½ teaspoon salt

Directions

Preheat the oven to 350F and prepare a 13x9 inch pan by greasing or with cooking spray. Melt the butter over a low heat and set aside to cool. Add the sugar, molasses, eggs and vanilla to a bowl and whisk together. In a separate bowl mix together the flour, salt, ginger, cinnamon and nutmeg. Slowly add the dry ingredients to the egg mix. Add the batter to the pan and cook for about 25 minutes. Remove and allow to cool in the pan. Slice and serve.

Oat and Blueberry Squares

Ingredients

1 cup rolled oats

¾ cup light brown sugar

1 cup all-purpose flour

½ cup butter

1 teaspoon cinnamon

1 package (8 ounce) cream cheese

½ cup granulated sugar

1 egg

3 tablespoons lemon juice

2 teaspoon vanilla extract

1 cup blueberries

Directions

Preheat the oven to 350F and prepare a 9x9 inch pan by greasing or with cooking spray. Add the oats, flour, cinnamon and brown sugar in a bowl and mix.

Add the butter, cut into small pieces and mix again until the mixture is like crumbs. Add half the mixture to the pan and cook for about 10 minutes. Remove and allow to cool.

Add the cream cheese and sugar into a bowl and mix. Then add the egg, lemon juice and vanilla extract and beat until smooth. Add in the blueberries and then pour the batter over the pan. Sprinkle the remaining half of the crumbly mixture over the top.

Place the pan back into the oven and cook for another 3 minutes or until it is golden. Remove from heat and allow to cool before cutting into squares to serve.

Oatmeal and Fudge Bars

Ingredients

1 cup butter

2 cups brown sugar

2 eggs

2 teaspoons vanilla

1 teaspoon almond extract

3 cups rolled oats

2 ½ cups all-purpose flour

1 cup sliced almonds (optional)

1 teaspoon baking soda

½ teaspoon salt

Filling

1 ½ cups semisweet chocolate chips

1 can (14 ounce) condensed milk

2 tablespoons butter

½ teaspoon salt

2 teaspoons vanilla

1 teaspoon almond extract

Directions

Preheat oven to 350F. Prepare a 15x10 pan by greasing the inside. Add 1 cup butter and the brown sugar to a bowl and beat together. Add in the eggs, vanilla and almond extract and mix in. In a new bowl, add the oats, flour, almonds, baking soda and salt and mix together. Add a little more than half of the mixture into the pan and press down with your hands to compact it.

In a saucepan over a low heat, add the chocolate chips, condensed milk, butter and salt. Heat until the mixture is smooth. Take off the heat and add the vanilla and almond extracts. Pour the chocolate mixture over the pan and then add the rest of the mixture on top.

Bake for about 25 minutes or until a toothpick comes out clean. Remove from the oven, allow to cool and cut into squares to serve.

Oatmeal Sheet Cake

Ingredients

1 cup oats

1 ½ cups hot water

½ cup butter

1 cup brown sugar

1 cup white sugar

2 eggs

1 ½ cups all-purpose flour

1 teaspoon baking soda

1 teaspoon cinnamon

½ teaspoon salt

Icing

½ cup butter

1 cup brown sugar

1 tablespoon milk

1 cup coconut

Directions

Preheat the oven to 350F and prepare a 13x9 inch pan by greasing or with cooking spray. Add the water to the oatmeal and set aside while you make the rest. In another bowl, add the butter and sugars and cream them together. Beat in the eggs one at a time and set aside. In a different bowl again, mix in the flour cinnamon, baking soda and salt. Add half of the flour mix to the butter mixture and now add in the oatmeal. Finish by adding in the rest of the flour and mixing well.

Add the mixture to the pre-prepared pan and bake for about 35 minutes. Remove and allow to cool.

To make the icing, add butter, brown sugar and milk into your saucepan and bring to the boil. After a minute add in the coconut and spread over the cake to serve.

Oaty Raisin Bars

These are tasty and versatile. I've added raisins, but you can try a great variety of extras for flavor from dates to figs to chocolate chips. Any type of fruit will work well with these.

Ingredients

1 cup butter

¾ cup sugar

¾ cup brown sugar

3 cups rolled oats

1 ½ cups all-purpose flour

1 teaspoon baking powder

1 teaspoon salt

2 cups raisins

2 eggs

2 teaspoons vanilla

Directions

Preheat the oven to 350F and prepare a 13x9 inch pan by greasing or with cooking spray. Add the butter with the sugars and combine. Add in the oats, flour, baking powder and salt and combine again. Add in the raisins, eggs and vanilla and mix. Add the batter to the pan and bake for about 30 minutes or until a toothpick comes out clean.

Orange Sheet Cake with Orange Cream Cheese Icing

This is very easy to make and the buttermilk keeps it lovely and moist. This cake has a nice subtle, orange flavour to it that's not overpowering but is very refreshing.

Ingredients

2 ½ cups all-purpose flour

2 teaspoons vanilla

2 tablespoons orange zest

1 tablespoon baking powder

½ teaspoon salt

1 cup butter

1 ½ cups sugar

3 eggs

½ teaspoon orange extract

1 cup buttermilk

Icing

½ cup butter

2 packs cream cheese

3 tablespoons orange juice

2 tablespoons orange zest

3 cups powdered sugar

Directions

Preheat your oven to 350F. Add the flour, orange zest, baking powder and salt into a bowl and mix together. In a new bowl, add the sugar gradually and continue to beat in.

Add the eggs individually and beat the mixture each time before adding the orange extract and vanilla. Add in the flour and buttermilk and add to the pan. Cook for about 25 minutes and allow to cool in the pan for an hour.

For the icing add the butter, cream cheese, orange juice and orange zest into a bowl and mix together. Add in the sugar slowly continuing to beat. If it's a little too thick, you can add water. If it's too runny, then just add some more sugar. Spread on the cake and serve.

Peanut Butter Sheet Cake

Peanut butter lovers rejoice! This one is for you.

Ingredients

¼ cup creamy peanut butter

2 cups al-purpose flour

2 cups sugar

½ teaspoon baking soda

1 cup water

2 eggs

1 cup butter

1 teaspoon vanilla

½ cup buttermilk

Frosting

½ cup creamy peanut butter

¾ cup butter

6 tablespoons milk

3 cups powdered sugar

1 teaspoon vanilla

Directions

Preheat oven to 350 degrees and prepare a 15x10 pan by greasing it and optionally adding parchment paper or aluminium foil. Add together the flour, sugar, salt and baking soda and combine. Place the butter, water and peanut butter into a saucepan over a gentle heat and bring to the boil. Add the contents of the saucepan into the flour mixture. Now combine the vanilla, beaten eggs and buttermilk and add to the mixture.

Spread into your prepared pan and bake for around 25 minutes or until you get the browed appearance on top. Remove and allow to cool.

For the icing, combine the butter and milk and heat until melted. Add in the peanut butter, powdered sugar, vanilla and milk and mix. Spread on your cake and serve!

Pear Sheet Cake

This is a great recipe, especially if you have over-ripe pears in the house. I've put down 6 pears, but you could put 8 in if you're a big pear fan (as I am!).

Ingredients

6 ripe pears

½ cup granulated sugar

1 cup brown sugar

2/3 cup vegetable oil

2 eggs

3 cups all-purpose flour

½ teaspoon salt

2 teaspoons baking soda

2 teaspoons cinnamon

1 teaspoon vanilla extract

Directions

Preheat the oven to 350F and prepare a 13x9 inch pan by greasing or with cooking spray. Peel your overripe pears and slice them very thinly. Place them in a bowl and add in the sugars. Leave them there for an hour or so and then blend so everything is smooth.

Add in the flour, salt, baking soda and cinnamon into a separate bowl and blend together. Add the flour mixture to the pears and then add the oil, eggs and vanilla

Pour the batter into the pan and bake for about 75 minutes or until a toothpick comes out clean. Remove and cool before cutting into squares to serve.

Pecan Pie Bars

Ingredients

3 cups all-purpose flour

½ cup light brown sugar

Pinch of salt

1 cup butter

4 eggs

1 ½ cups corn syrup

½ cups sugar

½ cup brown sugar

3 tablespoons butter

2 teaspoons vanilla extract

3 cups pecans

Directions

Preheat oven to 350F. Prepare a 15x10 pan by greasing the inside. Add the flour, ½ cup brown sugar and salt. Mix until it becomes crumb like and add to the pan. Press down with your hand so it is even and compacted. Add to the oven and bake for 15 minutes.

In another bowl add the eggs, corn syrup, ½ cup white sugar, ½ cup brown sugar, 3 tablespoons butter and vanilla. You can toast the pecans first if you prefer them that way or just add them now. Once you have removed the pan, spread the batter evenly over the crust. Bake for a further 40 minutes and remove to cut into squares and serve.

Pineapple Sheet Cake

This pineapple cake is very quick to make and tastes delicious. It will disappear just as quickly at any gathering!

Ingredients

2 cups all-purpose flour

2 cups sugar

2 eggs

2 teaspoons baking soda

½ teaspoon salt

1 ½ teaspoons vanilla

1 can crushed pineapple

Icing

1 (8oz) cream cheese

¼ cup of butter

3 cups powdered sugar

2 teaspoon vanilla

Directions

Preheat your oven to 350F and prepare a greased 15x10 inch pan. Add all the ingredients for the cake into a large bowl and beat until the mixture is smooth. Bake for around 30-35 minutes or until a toothpick comes out clean and allow to cool.

For the frosting, add the butter to the cream cheese and beat. Add the powdered sugar and vanilla, mix in and then frost the cake to serve.

Pumpkin Sheet Cake

Ingredients

1 cup sugar

½ cup vegetable oil

1 teaspoon pumpkin spice

3 eggs

2 cups all-purpose flour

2 teaspoons baking soda

1 teaspoons ground cinnamon

½ teaspoon salt

1 (8oz) cream cheese

¼ cup of butter

3 cups powdered sugar

2 teaspoon vanilla

Directions

Add the pumpkin, sugar and oil into a bowl and mix together. Add the eggs and continue to mix. In a separate bowl combine the flour, baking soda, cinnamon, pumpkin spice and salt. Add this bowl to the egg bowl and beat. Pour the mixture into a pre-prepared 15x10 pan. Bake for around 25 minutes.

For the frosting, add the butter to the cream cheese and beat. Add the powdered sugar and vanilla, mix in and then frost the cake to serve.

Raspberry Crumble Bars

Ingredients

1 cup butter

2 1/2 cups all-purpose flour

½ cup sugar

½ cup light brown sugar

1 ½ cup oats

½ teaspoon salt

1 egg

1 jar raspberry jam

Directions

Preheat the oven to 350F and prepare a 13x9 inch pan by greasing or with cooking spray. Add the flour, sugars, oats, salt, butter and egg to a large bowl and beat together. Remove two cups of this crumb mixture and put to one side.

Spread the rest of the mixture on the bottom of the pan and press it down with your fingers. Using a spatula, gently spread the jam on top of the mixture so it is all covered. Finally, add the crumb mixture you previously set aside on the top and press lightly down again with your hands.

Bake for about 40 minutes or until lightly browned. Remove from the heat, allow to cool in the pan and cut into squares to serve.

Simple Vanilla Sheet Cake

Ingredients

2 ½ cups all-purpose flour

1 ½ cups sugar

½ cup butter

½ cup vegetable oil

1 cup water

2 teaspoons vanilla

1 teaspoon cinnamon

2 teaspoons baking soda

1 cup buttermilk

Icing

1 (8oz) cream cheese

¼ cup of butter

3 cups powdered sugar

2 teaspoon vanilla

Directions

Preheat the oven to 350F and prepare a 13x9 inch pan by greasing or with cooking spray. Add the flour and sugar together in a large bowl, mix together and set aside. Add the butter, oil and water to a saucepan and bring to the boil.

Add this to the flour mixture and beat everything together. Now beat in the eggs one at a time. Add in the vanilla, cinnamon, baking soda and buttermilk and beat again. Add the mixture to the pan and bake for about 20 minutes. Remove and allow to cool.

For the frosting, add the butter to the cream cheese and beat. Add the powdered sugar and vanilla, mix in and then frost the cake to serve.

Smore's Bars

Ingredients

2/3 cup light corn syrup

2 tablespoons butter

1 teaspoon vanilla

2 cups semisweet chocolate chips

8 cups honey graham cereal

2 cups miniature marshmallows

Directions

Prepare a 13x9 pan by greasing the inside. Add the corn syrup and butter into a saucepan and bring to the boil. Remove from the heat and add in the chocolate chips, stirring until fully melted in. Add the vanilla. Add the cereal into a large bowl and pour the chocolate mixture over the top making sure it is all coated. Add in the marshmallows and mix again.

Pour the mixture into the pan and place in the fridge until firm. Remove to cut into squares and serve.

Strawberry Sheet Cake

Ingredients

1 cup butter

1 ½ cups sugar

2 eggs

2 teaspoons lemon juice

1 teaspoon vanilla

2 cups all-purpose flour

2 tablespoons strawberry-flavored gelatin

½ teaspoon baking soda

¼ teaspoon salt

1 cup buttermilk

1 cup chopped strawberries

Icing

1 (8oz) cream cheese

¼ cup of butter

3 cups powdered sugar

2 teaspoon vanilla

Directions

Preheat the oven to 350F and prepare a 13x9 inch pan by greasing or with cooking spray. Add the sugar and butter together into a bowl and beat until fluffy. Add the eggs one at a time and beat after each one. Add the lemon juice and vanilla and beat again.

In another bowl, add the flour, gelatin, baking soda and salt and stir together. Add these dry ingredients to the egg mixture, followed by the buttermilk and beat again. Now stir in all the strawberries. Pour the batter into your pan.

Bake for around 30 minutes or until a toothpick emerges clean. Remove from oven and allow to cool for an hour. For the frosting, add the butter to the cream cheese and beat. Add the powdered sugar and vanilla, mix in and then frost the cake. Add some sliced strawberries for decoration and serve.

Sugar Cookie Bars

This is a very simple recipe which you can play around with as well yourself. If you switch the vanilla to maple syrup or perhaps almond extract, you can get a variety of flavors through a little experimentation.

Ingredients

1 cup butter

1 ½ cups sugar

4 eggs

3 teaspoons vanilla

2 cups all-purpose flour

½ teaspoon salt

Directions

Preheat the oven to 350F and prepare a 13x9 inch pan by greasing or with cooking spray. Melt the butter over a low heat and set aside to cool. Add the sugar, eggs and vanilla to a bowl and whisk together. Slowly stir in the flour and salt. Add the batter to the pan and cook for about 25 minutes. Remove and allow to cool in the pan. Slice and serve.

Sweet Potato and Cream Cheese Frosting Sheet Cake

If you have any leftover, cooked sweet potato that you're wondering what to do with, then wonder no more as this is your perfect recipe. Read on to turn your remaining vegetables into a lovely, spiced sheet cake.

Ingredients

4 eggs

2 cups sugar

1 ½ cups vegetable oil

2 cups all-purpose flour

2 tablespoons cinnamon

2 teaspoons baking powder

2-cups mashed, cooked sweet potato

Icing

1 (8oz) cream cheese

¼ cup of butter

3 cups powdered sugar

2 teaspoon vanilla

Directions

Preheat your oven to 350F and prepare your 13x9 pan by greasing with optional parchment paper. Add the oil, sugar and eggs into a large bowl and whisk. Set aside. In a separate bowl, stir the flour, baking powder and cinnamon together.

Add this bowl to the egg mixture bowl and whisk all together. Now continue to whisk in the sweet potato.

Add your completed mixture into the prepared pan and cook for around 25 minutes. Remove from the oven and cool for an hour or so.

To make the icing, add the butter to the cream cheese and beat. Add the powdered sugar and vanilla, mix in and then frost the cake. Add your pecans in whatever configuration you like for garnish.

Tandy Cake Sheet Cake

This one might take a little longer than the rest to make, but it really does look beautiful with its layers and will rapidly become a family favorite.

Ingredients

1 ½ cups sugar

4 eggs

1 ½ teaspoon vanilla

2 cups all-purpose flour

2 teaspoons baking powder

½ teaspoon salt

1 cup milk

2 tablespoons butter

Peanut butter to spread

1 pound chopped milk chocolate candy bar

Directions

Preheat oven to 350F and prepare a greased 15x10 inch pan. Add together the flour, salt and baking powder in a bowl and put aside. In a different bowl, combine the eggs, sugar and vanilla and beat together.

Add the flour mixture from the other bowl and beat in. Heat the butter and milk for a minute until all liquefied and add into the mixture.

Pour into the pan and cook for about 20 minutes or until the cake tester shows it is done. Remove from the oven and allow to cool.

For the layers, add peanut butter to taste first all over the cake. Place the cake in the fridge for about an hour. Melt your chocolate bars and then spread all over the peanut butter creating a lovely layered effect. Allow to cool and serve.

Texas Sheet Cake

Ingredients

1 cup butter

1 cup water

2 cups all-purpose flour

1 1/2 cup sugar

3 tablespoons baking cocoa

1 teaspoon baking soda

½ teaspoon salt

½ cup buttermilk

2 eggs, beaten

1 teaspoon vanilla

Icing

½ cup butter

6 tablespoons milk

3 tablespoons cocoa

3 cups powdered sugar

1 teaspoon vanilla

1 cup pecans, chopped

Directions

Preheat your oven to 350F and prepare a 15x10x1 pan by greasing and adding parchment paper if you prefer. Add the flour, sugar and salt into a bowl and mix together. Add the butter, water and cocoa into a saucepan and bring to the boil. Pour it all over the flour mix and stir. Add the buttermilk, baking soda, vanilla and eggs and stir.

Add the mixture into your pan and bake for about 20 to 25 minutes. Remove from the oven and allow to cool for an hour or so or until it is gently warm to the touch.

For the frosting, heat the butter, a further 3 tablespoons of cocoa and the milk until it simmers. Take the pan off the heat and beat the powdered sugar and vanilla in. Now add the pecans. Pour over the cake, let it cool so the frosting hardens and serve.

Toffee Cinnamon Bars

Ingredients

½ cup butter

1 ½ cups brown sugar

2 eggs

2 teaspoons vanilla

2 cups all-purpose flour

2 teaspoons baking soda

2 teaspoons cinnamon

12 ounces semisweet chocolate chips

Directions

Prepare a 13x9 pan by greasing the inside. Place the butter and sugar into a saucepan and bring it to the boil. Remove and set aside to cool. Add it to a large bowl, followed by the eggs and vanilla. In a separate bowl, add the flour, baking powder and cinnamon and then slowly add to the eggs and mix. Add the chocolate chips and mix again.

Pour the batter into the pan and bake for 25 minutes. Remove, allow to cool and cut into squares to serve.

Very Easy Granola Bars

Ingredients

2 cups rolled oats

¾ cup crunchy peanut butter

½ cup ground flaxseed

1 teaspoon cinnamon

½ teaspoon salt

¾ cup raisins (or any fruit you like)

½ cup semi-sweet choc chips

¾ cup honey

¼ cup chopped almonds or peanuts

Directions

Add the oats, peanut butter, flaxseed, cinnamon, salt, honey, raisins, chocolate chips and almonds into a bowl and stir together. Add the mixture to a 11x9 dish and use your hands or a spatula to press down. Place in the fridge for 2 hours, cut into squares and serve!

White Chocolate and Macadamia Bars

Ingredients

1 cup butter

¾ cup granulated sugar

¾ cup brown sugar

3 eggs

2 ½ cups all-purpose flour

1 teaspoon baking soda

½ teaspoon salt

1 teaspoon vanilla

1 cup white chocolate chips

1 cup crushed macadamia nuts

Directions

Preheat the oven to 350F and prepare a 13x9 inch pan by greasing or with cooking spray. Add the butter and sugars to a bowl and beat until fluffy. Add the eggs and vanilla and beat again. Add the flour, baking soda and salt and beat again. Add in the white chips and macadamia nuts. Stir and then add the batter to the pan.

Cook for about 35 minutes or until a toothpick comes out clean. Remove from heat, allow to cool and cut to taste for serving.

White Texas Sheet Cake

Ingredients

2 cups all-purpose flour

1 cup butter

1 cup water

1 ½ cups sugar

2 eggs

½ cup sour cream

1 teaspoon almond extract

½ teaspoon salt

1 teaspoon baking soda

Icing

½ cup butter

¼ cup milk

4 cups powdered sugar

1 teaspoon almond extract

Directions

Preheat your oven to 375F and prepare a 15x10 pan either by greasing it or using parchment paper. Add the butter and water into a pan and bring to a boil.

Remove from the heat and then add in the flour, sugar, eggs, almond extract, baking soda, sour cream and salt. Stir until the mixture is smooth and add it all to your pan.

Bake for about 20 minutes and then let it cool for no more than 30 minutes so it is still warm. For the icing, add the butter and milk into a pan and bring to the boil. Now add the sugar with the almond extract and mix. Add the icing onto your cake and serve. You can also add some nuts for decoration if you like.

Zucchini Sheet Cake

Ingredients

1/2 cup vegetable oil

2 cups sugar

3 eggs

2 teaspoons vanilla

2 ½ cups all-purpose flour

½ teaspoon baking powder

2 teaspoons baking soda

1 teaspoon cinnamon

½ teaspoon salt

2 cups grated zucchini

Icing

½ cup butter

1 packet cream cheese (3 ounce)

1 ½ cups powdered sugar

Directions

Preheat oven to 350F. Prepare a 13x9 pan by greasing the inside. Add the eggs, sugar and vanilla into a large bowl and mix together. In a separate bowl and the flour, baking powder, cinnamon, baking soda and salt and combine.

Stir the flour mixture into the eggs. Squeeze the zucchini to ensure the liquid is drained and add into the mix. Pour into the pre-prepared pan.

Bake for about 25 minutes or until a toothpick emerges clean. Remove and allow to cool. Add the remaining butter, cream cheese and sugar into a bowl and mix together. Spread over the cake and serve!

More books by the Author

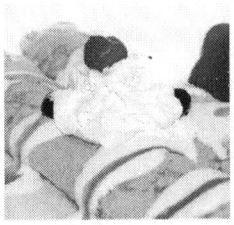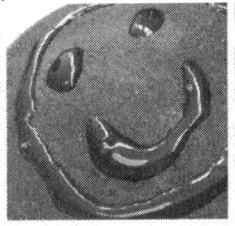

PANCAKE COOKBOOK

TOP 50 PANCAKE RECIPES

JULIE BROOKE

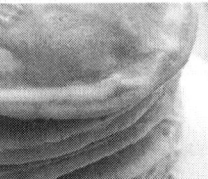

Fudge Cookbook

TOP 60 FUDGE RECIPES

Julie Brooke

Printed in Great Britain
by Amazon

28340545R00044